Beer Country's

BLACKOUTS & BOEREWORS

Karl Tessendorf and Greg Gilowey

My Fellow South Africans,

Load-shedding sucks! You know it. We know it. The whole country knows it. It's also no secret that it's here to stay for the foreseeable future. Is it annoying, frustrating and downright infuriating? Yes, no question about it.

But what if we told you that it doesn't have to be? What if we told you that you're gifted an opportunity with every flick of the substation switch? The opportunity to light a fire and do what South Africans do best - braai!

Every blackout is a fire begging to be built, a juicy chop ready to be turned, and a family braai just waiting to happen. So join us as we flip the script on the aggravation of load-shedding and braai our way through whatever stage comes our way.

With a little planning, some clever thinking, and a few great recipes, load-shedding can go from the worst part of your day to the best. Don't believe us? Then put your money where your braaibroodjie goes, and join us as we dive into our best braai recipes for the Eishkom disaster. Welcome to the braaight side of load-shedding life!

Ministers of Non-electrical Cooking
Department of Fire and Smoke
@BeerCountrySA

Published in 2023 by Penguin Books, an imprint
of Penguin Random House South Africa (Pty) Ltd
Company Reg. No. 1953/000441/07
The Estuaries, 4 Oxbow Crescent, Century Avenue,
Century City 7441, Cape Town, South Africa
PO Box 1144, Cape Town, 8000, South Africa

www.penguinrandomhouse.co.za

ISBN 978-1-48590-185-3

Publisher: Beverley Dodd
Managing editor: Aimee Sinclair
Designer: Randall Watson
Editor and indexer: Linda de Villiers
Proofreader: Cecilia Barfield
Photographer: Henk Hattingh
Photographer's assistant: Stefan Venter
Stylist: Caro Gardner
Stylist's Assistant: Elizma Voigt

Reproduction: Studio Repro, Cape Town

Printed by
novus print
A division of Novus Holdings

CONTENTS

THIS IS GREG

It's another crazy day here in Mzanzi, liberally seasoned with some load-shedding lunacy. But for me, this blackout batshittery ain't all boredom and burnt braaibroodjies. Our daily digital detox really can be more of a blessing than a curse if we use it to learn, to laugh, to bond, and yes absolutely, to braai. It's distraction-free quality time, gifted in a shiny silver braaibak.

My two daughters can now build and light the braai, set up camp, tie ten knots, cook a killer boerie roll, bake bread, pick mussels off the rocks, grow herbs and veggies, pickle onions, play vinyl records, and bleed the brakes on my old Landy. My youngest even knows how to make cider from apple juice. I'm pretty sure that ain't the best parenting on the planet but if the zombie apocalypse hits, they'll be on the A-Team for sure.

I guess what I'm saying is that down here in the wild, wild South, even when days are dark, we fight for the bright side - we *maak 'n plan*. We rely on our military-grade sense of humour forged in our country's crucible of chaos and smile as we look to our leaders with a raised middle finger and loudly proclaim, 'No power, no problem!' So here's hoping these few recipes help make the darkness a little lighter, and the braais a little brighter. Cheers!

THIS IS KARL

Aaah, load-shedding! My favourite part of the day – said no one ever. Remember when it was just once a day? Those were good times that we took for granted… I don't know about you, but these days, even with the reminder apps I still get caught out by the ever-changing schedule. When darkness descends, there's usually a split-second realisation followed by a loud 'F@#K!'. And no matter how often it happens, I never seem to get used to it.

Imagine if scientists could harness the collective power of all the 'F@#Ks' shouted with each load-shed. We'd never have an electricity problem again. While I can't help you deal with the daily annoyance of load-shedding, I can offer tasty ideas on how to use the downtime. This short, sharp and snappy little braai book is packed with great recipes, awesome flavour-bomb ideas, and a little pantry wisdom.

Sure, there's some planning involved, but your efforts will be rewarded with epic braai chow. So let's take a half-beer-glass-full approach to the unending blackouts and turn that 'F@#K!' into 'F@#K yeah! It's braai time!'.

MAKING FLAVOUR BOMBS

A killer sauce or condiment is one of the easiest ways to take your braai from good to great. Just ask the French (not that they braai much), whose incredible sauces are a huge part of their cuisine. A great sauce can lift a bland dish or add a one-two punch of spice and fresh herbs. A flavoured butter can level up your braaibroodjie game, and a slow-fermented dough will have your friends wondering why your roosterkoek are always better than theirs. In short, the better prepared you are, the better your braai will taste. Here are a few of our go-to favourites for just about every braai situation.

LIME SWEET CHILLI SAUCE

Proper sweet chilli sauce that's actually hot and great on anything.

½ C white sugar	4 cloves garlic, chopped	1 Tbsp cornflour mixed with
¾ C water	A big knob of fresh ginger,	1 Tbsp cold water
¼ C rice vinegar	peeled and chopped	Zest of 2 limes
2 Tbsp fish sauce	15-20 long red chillies, chopped	

Add all the ingredients except the cornflour, water and zest to a medium-size pot. Mix well and place over medium-high heat. Bring to a boil, then turn down the heat and simmer for 10 minutes. After 10 minutes, mix the cornflour and water together to form a slurry and add to the pot. Simmer for another 2 minutes to thicken, then remove from the heat and cool. Add the lime zest and blitz briefly with a stick blender to break down the chillies. Bottle and store in the fridge for up to a month.

TOMATO SMOOR

A versatile smoor to top, dip and slather on all your tasty boeries, burgers or any braai chow.

Olive oil	A knob of butter	½ C water
1 large onion, peeled and sliced	1 Tbsp dried mixed herbs	1 Tbsp sugar
3 cloves garlic, chopped	1 Tbsp paprika	1 Tbsp fish sauce
2 Tbsp tomato paste	2 tins (400 g each) whole peeled tomatoes, crushed	Sea salt and freshly ground black pepper

Set a pot or pan over medium heat. Heat a glug of olive oil and fry the onion until it softens and browns. Add the garlic, tomato paste and butter and stir-fry for 2-3 minutes. Add the herbs and paprika and fry for another minute until fragrant. Add the tomatoes, water, sugar and fish sauce and bring to a simmer. Cook, uncovered, until the liquid reduces and the smoor is thickened to your liking. Remove from the heat and season to taste. Store in the fridge for up to a week.

YOGHURT PESTO

Herby, creamy and delicious.

100 g pesto flavour of your choice
2 C double cream plain yoghurt

Sea salt and freshly ground
black pepper

Mix all the ingredients and season to taste. Use as a marinade and basting sauce for kebabs.

BEER COUNTRY'S
QUARTER CUP BRAAI MARINADE

Easy to remember, simple to make and super tasty on meat or veggies.

¼ C hoisin sauce
¼ C tomato sauce
¼ C Worcestershire sauce

¼ C sriracha sauce
¼ C Mrs Ball's chutney
¼ C beer

Zest and juice of 1 lime

Pop all the ingredients except the lime zest and juice into a small pot over medium heat. Whisk for 2-3 minutes to combine, then remove from the heat and add the zest and juice. Store in the fridge for up to two weeks.

GREEN HERB SAUCE

If your dish needs a bright, herby kick, this is the sauce for you.

1 C olive oil
4 anchovy fillets, finely chopped
2 Tbsp red wine vinegar
A big handful of fresh flat-
   leaf parsley, chopped

Zest and juice of 1 lemon
A big handful of fresh chives,
   chopped
A big handful of fresh basil,
   chopped

1 Tbsp baby capers
2 tsp Dijon mustard
1 clove garlic, chopped
Sea salt and freshly ground
   black pepper

Add all the ingredients to a mixing bowl, whisking well to combine, then season to taste. We like to chop everything by hand for a chunkier texture, but you can also blitz it with a hand blender for a smoother consistency. Store in the fridge for up to two weeks.

GREEN CHILLI SAUCE

A simple sauce that packs a Thai-inspired flavour explosion.

15 long green chillies, finely
   chopped
3 cloves garlic, finely chopped
¼ C olive oil

A knob of fresh ginger,
   peeled and finely chopped
Zest and juice of 1 lime
1 Tbsp fish sauce

1 tsp sugar
Sea salt and freshly ground
   black pepper

Add all the ingredients to a bowl and mix well to combine, then season to taste. Store in the fridge for up to two weeks.

QUICK PICKLED RED ONION

The most versatile garnish you'll ever make.

½ C red wine vinegar
¼ C water
2 Tbsp sugar

1 tsp salt
1 medium red onion, peeled and
  thinly sliced

(Add a few sliced chillies if
  you are feeling spicy)

Whisk the red wine vinegar, water, sugar and salt together in a small bowl to dissolve and combine. Submerge the onion, then set aside to pickle for at least 30 minutes before serving. Store in the fridge for up to two weeks.

MAKE-AHEAD DOUGH

Have epic roosterkoek dough on hand straight from your fridge.

500 g white bread wheat flour
350 g water
1 Tbsp olive oil

1 Tbsp sugar
5 g instant yeast
1 tsp salt

Add all the ingredients to a large mixing bowl and mix until no dry flour remains, then turn the dough out onto a work surface. Knead for 8-10 minutes, then place into an oiled bowl and cover. Rest on the counter for 1 hour, then place it in the fridge overnight or for up to 3 days. The next day, remove the dough from the fridge and let it warm up for an hour. Divide the dough into 8-10 equal-size portions and roll them into balls. Cover and let them proof for 30 minutes. Braai the roosterkoek over medium-heat coals, turning frequently. When the roosterkoek sound hollow when tapped with a finger they are done. Roosterkoek can take up to 20 minutes to bake, so plan accordingly.

COWBOY BUTTER

The internet's favourite cowboy butter is worthy of its praise.

250 g butter, softened
4 cloves garlic, finely
  chopped
Zest and juice of
  1 small lemon
1 Tbsp Dijon mustard

1 tsp chilli flakes
1 tsp paprika
½ tsp smoked paprika
½ tsp cayenne pepper
A small handful of fresh flat-
  leaf parsley, chopped

A small handful of fresh
  chives, chopped
5 sprigs of fresh thyme,
  picked and chopped
Sea salt and freshly ground
  black pepper

Mix all the ingredients for the butter and season to taste. Store in the fridge for daily use or roll it into a log with plastic wrap and store it in the freezer.

MISO BUTTER

Use on meat, veggies and for an instant umami boost.

---

250 g butter, softened
75 g miso paste
1 tsp honey

Zest of 1 lemon
Sea salt and freshly ground
   black pepper

Mix all the ingredients for the butter and season to taste. Store in the fridge for daily use or roll it into a log with plastic wrap and store it in the freezer.

PESTO BUTTER

Pick your pesto poison and pack flavour into any dish.

---

250 g butter, softened
100 g pesto flavour of your choice
Sea salt and freshly ground black pepper

Mix the butter and pesto and season to taste. Store in the fridge for daily use or roll it into a log with plastic wrap and store it in the freezer.

LABNEH

Labneh is strained yoghurt that's double thick and creamy. It's the perfect all-rounder dip that mixes well with everything from peri-peri sauce to pesto.

Muslin cloth or a clean piece
   of linen
A sieve or colander

1 kg double cream plain
   yoghurt
1 tsp salt

Zest of 2 lemons
Sea salt and freshly ground
   black pepper

Line the sieve or colander with a piece of muslin or linen and place it into a bowl. Mix the yoghurt, salt and lemon zest in a large mixing bowl, spoon it into the lined sieve and fold the muslin or linen over to cover. Refrigerate and let the yoghurt strain for 24 hours, then discard the liquid and decant the labneh into a container. Season to taste, cover and store refrigerated for up to two weeks.

EASY FRIDGE DRESSING

Dressing 101: 3 parts oil to 1 part acid; add extra flavour boosters and shake.

Base Ingredients
6 Tbsp olive oil
2 Tbsp acid (red wine, apple
   cider or balsamic vinegar,
   or lemon juice)
1 tsp Dijon mustard

Sea salt and freshly ground
   black pepper

Extra Flavour Boost Options
Chopped garlic

Chopped fresh herbs
Honey for sweetness
Labneh or double cream yoghurt
   for creaminess
Chilli flakes
Lemon zest

Add the base ingredients to a jar with a lid. Add your chosen flavour boosters. Close and shake. Store in the fridge for up to a week.

POWER UP YOUR PANTRY

Now that you're the king of condiments and the sultan of sauces, it's time to power up your pantry. With this store-bought collection of spices, smears, sauces and jazzer-uppers at the ready, you can say *tsek!* to bland braais. We've used many of these in our recipes, but feel free to play around. Mix and match flavours to create new combinations and become the master of your pantry universe.

ALL GOLD TOMATO SAUCE
It's great as is or perfect for adding sweetness and acidity to marinades, sauces or potjies.

CHAKALAKA
Chakalaka is tasty on anything. You can even blitz it up and use it as a marinade.

CHILLI CRISP
The king of crunch is good on everything from boeries, burgers and braaibroodjies to steaks, chops and salads. Or you can just eat it straight out of the jar.

DOUBLE CREAM PLAIN YOGHURT
Used to make its thicker cousin labneh, double cream yoghurt is a versatile kitchen ingredient. Use it in basting sauces, dressings, dips or as an overnight marinade with harissa that also tenderises meat.

DUKKAH OR ZA'ATAR
These Middle Eastern spice, seed and nut blends will add life, texture, crunch and spice to anything and everything.

EASY PANTRY BBQ SAUCE
½ C tomato sauce, ¼ C Mrs Balls Chutney, ¼ C hoisin sauce, ¼ C Worcestershire sauce, a big shake of Cape Herb & Spice Smokehouse BBQ. Mix it up, slather it on and braai!

FISH SAUCE
Fish sauce is a magical ingredient that we use in everything from sauces, marinades and dips to anything and everything in a potjie. Its natural umami makes everything taste more like it should.

GOOD QUALITY MAYONNAISE
Mayo is a wonder condiment. You can mix it with other condiments or blitz it with herbs to make sauces. You can use it instead of butter for your braaibroodjies and, in a pinch, you can even mix it with braai spice and use it as a basting marinade.

GREAT SPICE BLENDS
With so many incredible spice blends on the market these days, there's no excuse to use the same old braai salt that your ancestors used. We love Cape Herb & Spice Company's shaker tins for their punch and variety.

HARISSA
Packed with chillies, spices and herbs, harissa is a versatile all-rounder. Loosen with olive oil for basting, add to labneh to create a dip, or mix it with plain yoghurt for an epic braai marinade.

HOISIN SAUCE

This magical sauce comes from Chinese cooking and it's thick, dark, sweet, salty and savoury. It's excellent as a dipping sauce or marinade, and it mixes well with yoghurt or labneh.

LEMONS AND LIMES

Lemons and limes add flavour to any dish, but more importantly, they add acid. Acid makes flavours pop, especially when it hits that tasty, charred fat on a *tjoppie*. Use the zest for sprinkling and juice for squeezing.

MRS BALL'S CHUTNEY

You love it. We love it. South Africa loves it.

OLIVE OIL

Great olive oil is essential in any kitchen. Cook with it, dip stuff in it, drizzle it on everything, or use it as a final flourish to finish any dish.

PARMESAN

Much like Worcestershire, parmesan is packed with natural MSG. There aren't many dishes that don't benefit from a generous sprinkle of the good stuff.

PERI-PERI SAUCE

We'll be the first to admit that we have a peri-peri sauce problem. If we see a new one, we buy it immediately. That said, there's nothing wrong with a good ol' bottle of Nandos. You know what to do with this one.

PESTO

The original herb flavour bomb. Mix with olive oil to make a drizzle or basting, or stir into yoghurt for a dip.

WORCESTERSHIRE SAUCE

The real stuff is made from anchovies, so it's a pure natural MSG flavour bomb. It'll lift any sauce or marinade and add richness and depth to any potjie.

BEER COUNTRY'S LOAD-SHEDDING LEGENDS

If you've ever driven behind a taxi in South Africa, there's a good chance you've seen the slogan, 'when days are dark, friends are few' plastered on a back window. Well, we're happy to report that even though days are dark, we've still got amazing friends that we can count on. Without this collection of local legends, this load-shedding book would not have seen the light of day. So cheers to you, guys and gals!

DARLING BREW

Darling Brew is one of South Africa's best craft breweries and they've got a beer for everyone. If you ever find yourself in Darling, be sure to stop by their incredible facility and tell them we sent you.
www.darlingbrew.co.za

TJ'S LEKKA BRAAI

TJ's has been part of the Beer Country journey since the beginning and they're responsible for many a lekker braai. They've got all the wood, charcoal and firelighters you'll ever need plus a range of braai gear.
www.tjslekkabraai.co.za

CAPE HERB & SPICE

Cape Herb & Spice is your one-stop shop for all your spice flavour bomb needs. We use their rub shaker tins on everything and our braais are better for it. Find your favourite flavour today and get cooking!
www.capeherb.co.za

WÜSTHOF

We were Wüsthof fans before we wrote our first book and we're still fans three books later. Slice, dice and chop your way to great food with Wüsthof each and every time.
www.edisonstone.com

VICTORIA COOKWARE

Our favourite three-generation family-owned cast-iron business is back with more incredible pans. They're beautiful to look at, great for everything and will last many lifetimes.
www.edisonstone.com

BILL RILEY MEAT

Cape Town's favourite family butcher has been our family butcher since forever. They've always got what we need and their personal service makes all the difference.
www.billrileymeat.co.za

PENGUIN & OUR TEAM

Lastly, we'd like to give a big shout-out to Bev, Randall, Aimee, Linda, Cecilia, Caro, Henk, Stefan and Elizma. Without you guys and gals, this book would not have been possible. Thanks for all the hard work. We look forward to the next one!

RECIPES

STAGE 2: QUICK & EASY

SMOKY STEAK TACOS
WITH CHIPOTLE ESQUITES SALAD

This Mexican street-food classic gets a braaied taco supercharger.

Feeds: 4-6 • Prep: 20 minutes • Cook: 15 minutes

Chipotle Esquites Salad
4 corn cobs, husks removed
Olive oil
1 avo, peeled and diced
2 rounds of feta cheese, crumbled
2 spring onions, finely sliced
A small handful of fresh coriander, chopped
2 chipotle peppers in adobo, chopped
1 clove garlic, finely chopped
2-3 Tbsp mayonnaise
1 Tbsp paprika
Zest and juice of 1 lime
Sea salt and freshly ground black pepper

The Steak and Tacos
600 g rump or ribeye steak
Olive oil
Sea salt and freshly ground black pepper
  or your favourite braai spice
Flour or corn tortillas

To Serve
Green Chilli Sauce (see p. 7)
Lime wedges or halves

Drizzle the corn with some olive oil, then braai over high heat to char. When the cobs are charred on all sides, remove them from the heat and allow to cool. Slice the kernels off the cobs and place into a mixing bowl. Add the remaining salad ingredients and mix well. Season to taste and set aside.

Drizzle the steak with oil and season. Braai the steak over hot coals for 3-4 minutes per side or until the internal temperature hits 50 °C for medium-rare. Let the steak rest while you heat up the tortillas on the fire. Place the warm tortillas into a pot with a lid to keep them from drying out. Slice the steak thinly and season with salt and pepper.

To assemble, lay a few slices of steak on each tortilla, top with the esquites salad and drizzle over the Green Chilli Sauce. Serve with lime wedges or halves for squeezing.

BOERIE-STUFFED FRENCH BRAAIBROODJIES

Is it a boerie roll, or is it a braaibroodjie?
Who cares! It's so damn tasty and that's all that matters.

Feeds: 4-6 • Prep: 20 minutes • Cook: 10 minutes

The Broodjie
1 large French loaf,
  sliced in half horizontally
Butter, softened
Chutney
2 store-bought pickled onions, sliced
100 g mozzarella, sliced
600 g good quality thick boerewors
Olive oil

To Serve
Green Herb Sauce (see p. 7)
Or
Lime Sweet Chilli Sauce (see p. 6)

Start by scooping out the soft bread from the top and bottom of the French loaf. This makes it easier to nestle the ingredients into the bread. Brush each side with butter, then add a layer of chutney to each half. Sprinkle on the pickled onions, top with cheese and press them down.

Using a sharp knife, slice the wors skin, then peel it off and discard. It's easier if you slice the wors into manageable pieces. Drizzle a little olive oil onto your hands and flatten the wors meat on your work surface until it is almost the same width as the bread. Lift the meat off the work surface and pop it onto the bread. Use your thumbs to work it all the way to the edges of the bread. The meat will stop the edges of the bread from burning on the braai. Repeat this until you've used all the meat and have evenly covered the top and bottom halves of the loaf.

Place the loaves, meat-side down, onto a flip grid. Close it but don't secure it. Braai over medium-hot coals for 8-10 minutes until the meat is caramelised and the cheese melted. Flip the loaves and toast the underside of the bread for a minute before removing them from the braai. Pop the loaves onto a chopping board and top with Green Herb Sauce or Lime Sweet Chilli Sauce. Slice and serve immediately.

CHARRED BONE MARROW ON TOAST
WITH QUICK PICKLE SALAD

The best toast dinner you'll ever have.

Feeds: 4-6 • Prep: 40 minutes • Cook: 15 minutes

The Marrow and Toast

6 large marrow bone canoes
Olive oil
Sea salt and freshly ground black pepper
  or your favourite braai spice
8 slices of sourdough bread

The Salad

Quick Pickled Red Onion (see p. 8)
100 g wild rocket
½ C baby capers, roughly chopped
Zest and juice of 1 lemon
Olive oil

Drizzle the bones with olive oil and season with salt and pepper or your favourite braai spice. Braai the bones, marrow-side down, over hot coals for 1-2 minutes to caramelise, then flip them over. When the marrow starts to bubble, move them to a cooler part of the fire. Pop the sourdough onto the grill and toast both sides until golden. Set aside.

For the salad, remove the desired amount of pickled onion from the liquid and add it to a salad bowl with the rocket, capers, lemon juice and zest. Drizzle in enough olive oil just to coat, then toss well to combine.

To assemble, scoop the warm marrow onto the toast, top with handfuls of salad and tuck in.

CHORIZO BUTTER PRAWNS

A quick and easy flavour feast, and you're invited.

Feeds: 4 • Prep: 20 minutes • Cook: 12 minutes

---

1 kg king prawns, cleaned
Olive oil
200 g chorizo, chopped into small blocks
100 g Pesto Butter (see p. 9)
Sea salt and freshly ground black pepper
A handful of flat-leaf parsley, chopped

To Serve
Lemon wedges or thick slices

To clean the prawns, use a pair of kitchen scissors to snip open the shell along the back of the prawns. Use the tip of a sharp paring knife to carefully lift out the vein and discard. If you pierce the vein, you can rinse the prawn off with water to clean it. Drizzle the prawns with a little olive oil and set aside.

Set a cast-iron pan over medium-high-heat coals and heat the olive oil. Add the chorizo and fry until it is almost crispy. Add the Pesto Butter and fry for another 2 minutes until fragrant. Remove the pan from the heat and season to taste.

Season the prawns with salt and pepper, then pop them on the grill over medium-high-heat coals. Braai for 2-3 minutes per side until pink and charry. Brush the prawns with a little chorizo butter in the last minute of braaiing. Place the prawns into the warm butter and toss to combine. Garnish with flat-leaf parsley and serve with lemon wedges or slices.

STEAK PANZANELLA SALAD
WITH TOASTED CIABATTA

Fresh and vibrant with hearty slices of medium-rare steak.

Feeds: 4 • Prep: 20 minutes • Cook: 15 minutes

The Dressing
2 Tbsp finely chopped red onion
2 sprigs of fresh thyme, picked and chopped
1 clove garlic, finely chopped
1 tsp dried oregano
¼ C olive oil
1 Tbsp red wine vinegar
1 tsp Dijon mustard
Sea salt and freshly ground black pepper

The Salad
600 g mixed baby tomatoes, sliced into wedges
A handful of fresh basil, chopped
A handful of fresh chives, chopped
½ C baby capers
A small red onion, peeled and thinly sliced
½ C grated or shaved parmesan
Sea salt and freshly ground black pepper

The Steak and Ciabatta
600 g rump steak
Olive oil
Your favourite braai spice
6 slices of ciabatta, drizzled with olive oil
Sea salt and freshly ground black pepper

For the dressing, toss all the ingredients into a bowl and whisk to combine. Set aside.

For the salad, season the tomatoes with salt and place them into a colander over a bowl for 20 minutes. This will draw out some of their moisture, which will stop the salad from becoming too soggy.

Drizzle the steak with oil and season with your favourite braai spice. Braai the steak over hot coals for 4-5 minutes per side or until the internal temperature hits 50 ºC for a medium-rare steak. Let the steak rest for 10 minutes while you toast the bread and prep the salad.

Toast the bread over medium-heat coals until golden, then chop or tear it into bite-size chunks. Place the chunks into a large mixing bowl, add the tomatoes and the rest of the salad ingredients.

Drizzle on the desired amount of dressing, more salt and pepper if necessary, and toss to combine. Tip the salad out onto a serving platter. Slice the steak thinly and drizzle with dressing before topping the salad and serving.

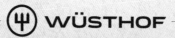

CAPRESE QUESADILLAS
WITH LIME SWEET CHILLI SAUCE

It's like a Caprese salad, but better because it's braaied.

Makes: 2 large quesadillas • Prep: 20 minutes • Cook: 10 minutes

---

The Tomatoes
300 g mixed baby tomatoes, diced
2 Tbsp balsamic vinegar
2 Tbsp olive oil
Zest of 1 lemon
Sea salt and freshly ground black pepper

The Quesadillas
4 large tortillas
300 g mozzarella, grated
Basil pesto, loosened with a little olive oil
Sea salt and freshly ground black pepper

To Serve
Lime Sweet Chilli Sauce (see p. 6)

Mix all the ingredients for the tomatoes, season to taste and set aside.

To assemble, you're going to build these on a flip grid, so lay two of the tortillas onto the grid. Add half of the cheese to both, top with tomatoes and dollops of basil pesto. Season with salt and freshly ground black pepper. Top with the remaining cheese, then top each with a second tortilla and secure the flip grid.

Braai over medium-heat coals until the tortillas are toasted and the cheese is melted. Transfer them to a cutting board, slice, garnish as desired and serve with Lime Sweet Chilli Sauce on the side.

BLACKENED CAJUN TUNA
WITH BRAAIED ROTIS AND GREEN CHILLI

Tear 'em up, fill 'em up, fold 'em up, and smash the best braaied tuna roti of your life.

Feeds: 4-6 • Prep: 10 minutes • Cook: 5 minutes

The Rotis
4 large store-bought rotis
  (get the real deal from your
  local Cape Malay or Indian takeaway)

The Green Chilli Sauce
(see p. 7)

The Tuna
600 g fresh line-caught tuna
Olive oil
Cape Herb & Spice Louisiana Cajun Rub

The Toppings
Rainbow slaw mix
Kewpie mayonnaise
2 spring onions, thinly sliced
2 Tbsp sesame seeds, toasted

Roughly tear the rotis into quarters. Stack them on a plate next to the braai so they're ready to toast when the tuna is done.

Make the Green Chilli Sauce by following the instructions on page 7.

Drizzle the tuna with oil and season well with Cajun rub. Place the tuna in a flip grid but don't close it. Just use the grid to flip it without squashing it. Braai the tuna over very hot coals for 30 seconds a side for a total of 2 minutes. If you are feeling brave, throw in a few pieces of kindling sticks to get some flame action going as you braai. Remove the tuna from the braai.

Spread the coals or adjust your grill height to drop the temperature for the rotis. Toast the rotis for approximately a minute per side until they are toasty but still soft. Slice the tuna and adjust the seasoning if necessary.

To assemble, top each roti with slaw and tuna slices. Drizzle with mayonnaise and finish with Green Chilli Sauce, spring onions, sesame seeds and any other green garnish, if you like.

BEER COUNTRY'S DRUMSTICKS
WITH GREEN CHILLI SAUCE

Clucking good chicken lollipops.

Feeds: 6 • Prep: 20 minutes • Cook: 30 minutes

**Beer Country's Quarter Cup
  Braai Marinade**
(see p. 7)

Green Chilli Sauce
(see p. 7)

The Drumsticks
20 free-range drumsticks
Olive oil
Your favourite braai spice

To Serve
A handful of chopped chives or
  your choice of other green garnish
Toasted sesame seeds
Lime wedges or slices

Make the Beer Country's Quarter Cup Braai Marinade and the Green Chilli Sauce according to the instructions, both on page 7.

Drizzle the drumsticks with oil and season with your favourite braai spice.

Arrange the drums on a flip grid and place it over medium-hot coals. Braai the chicken for 5 minutes per side to caramelise and char. After 5 minutes, baste the chicken with the braai marinade and continue braaiing for 3-4 minutes per side, basting the chicken with each flip to build up a caramelised layer of sauce. After 25-30 minutes, the drumsticks should be lekker sticky, dark and cooked through.

Arrange the chicken on a serving platter and top with chives or other garnish and sesame seeds. Serve with lime wedges or slices and Green Chilli Sauce, and attack!

KEBAB 101 THREE WAYS

Kebabs, sosaties, meat on a stick or whatever you call them,
they're always a braai-time winner.

Feeds: as many as you make • Prep: 20 minutes • Cook: 10-15 minutes

The Basics
Beef, chicken or lamb, cut into strips or chunks
Red onion, red or yellow peppers or dried fruit,
  cut into bite-size pieces
Kebab sticks, soaked in water
Olive oil
Sea salt and freshly ground black pepper
  or your favourite braai spice

Welcome to kebab 101! In this short tutorial, you'll learn a few tips and tricks on how to get the best out of our spiky friends. Let's get to it.

When it comes to meat, there are two routes to go. The first is to cut the meat into chunks or cubes. The second is to cut it into strips. The chunks go onto the kebabs sticks as is, but the strips need to be threaded like an accordion. Both work well but accordion threading gives you more nooks and crannies, which leads to more tasty caramelised edges. Also, remember that the larger the chunks of meat, the longer the kebabs will take to cook. Try both methods and see which floats your ke-boat.

A good kebab always has veg or fruit between the meat pieces. Red onion or peppers are classic, but feel free to mix it up with different veggie choices. Dried fruit is also great if you want a hint of sweetness, or if you're going the traditional curry sosatie route.

We like to braai kebabs over high heat and flip them often to build up a lekker caramelised crust. If you've pre-marinated the kebabs in barbecue sauce or anything with a lot of sugar, braai them over medium-heat coals to prevent burning. Remember to baste as you turn and always soak the sticks in water beforehand to prevent burning.

Below are a few tasty options to kickstart your kebab journey.

BEER COUNTRY'S QUARTER CUP BRAAI MARINADE (see p. 7)
Great on any meat.

LIME SWEET CHILLI SAUCE (see p. 6) **OR GREEN CHILLI SAUCE** (see p. 7)
Brush on towards the end of cooking and serve on the side.

YOGHURT PESTO (see p. 7)
Awesome on chicken or lamb.

PESTO PORK ESPETADAS TWO WAYS

Pesto is pure flavour in a bottle and we're in the flavour business, baby.

Feeds: 4-6 • Prep: 20 minutes • Cook: 15 minutes

The Chipotle Sundried Tomato Pesto
100 g sundried tomato pesto
2-3 chipotle peppers, finely chopped
Olive oil

The Green Chilli Basil Pesto
100 g basil pesto
¼ C Green Chilli Sauce (see p. 7)
Olive oil

The Pork
4 kg pork neck steaks
2 large skewers
Sea salt and freshly ground black pepper

For the pestos, mix the ingredients in two separate bowls, then drizzle in enough olive oil to create a semi-loose paste.

Divide the pork neck steaks into two equal piles. Slice the steaks into 2 cm-thick strips. Toss one pile in half of the chipotle sundried tomato pesto and the other half in the green chilli basil pesto and mix well to combine. To build the espetadas, thread the strips onto the two skewers like an accordion. Pack the pieces nice and tight so that they form a cohesive kebab. Once you've built both espetadas, season with salt and pepper. You could even do this in advance and let them marinate overnight in the fridge.

Braai the espetadas over hot coals for 2-3 minutes per side to caramelise and char. Brush the espetadas with the remaining marinades and continue cooking for another 4-5 minutes, flipping occasionally. Let the espetadas rest for at least 5 minutes before devouring. These go great with Roosterkoek (see p. 53).

MISO BUTTER MUSSELS
WITH GREMOLATA AND TOASTED CIABATTA

A mussel umami butter bomb that'll have you slurping
and smacking your lips in satisfaction.

Feeds: 4-6 • Prep: 20 minutes • Cook: 15 minutes

Gremolata
A handful of fresh flat-leaf parsley,
  washed and dried
1 clove garlic, finely minced
Zest of 2 lemons

The Mussels
Olive oil
1 large onion, peeled and chopped
4 cloves garlic, chopped
½ C lager
800 g half-shell mussels, sustainably farmed
400 g mussel meat, sustainably farmed
200 g Miso Butter (see p. 9)
Sea salt and freshly ground black pepper

The Bread
1 large ciabatta
Sea salt and freshly ground black pepper

Using a sharp chef's knife, chop the parsley until it's almost finely chopped. Add the minced garlic to the parsley, then sprinkle the lemon zest over the top. Mix the three on the chopping board to combine and give it a final chop to finish. Scoop it into a bowl and set aside.

For the mussels, preheat a large flat pot or number 3 potjie over medium-heat coals. Heat a glug of oil and fry the onion until it softens and browns. Toss in the garlic and fry for a minute until fragrant. Pour in the lager, cover and bring it to a boil. Add the mussels and mussel meat then cover again and steam for 5 minutes. After 5 minutes, add the butter and cover to melt. After the butter has melted, stir well to combine and remove from the heat. Season to taste.

Toast the ciabatta whole over the coals, then tear it into chunks. Serve the buttery mussels with the gremolata for sprinkling and the bread for scooping.

BRAAIED CABBAGE
WITH MISO BUTTER AND DUKKAH

If you've never had charred cabbage, there's no time like the present.

Feeds: 4-6 • Prep: 10 minutes • Cook: 15 minutes

The Butter
200 g Miso Butter (see p. 9), melted

The Cabbage
3 baby green cabbages
3 baby red cabbages
Olive oil
Sea salt and freshly ground black pepper

To Serve
Store-bought dukkah
Lemon wedges

Make the Miso Butter by following the instructions on page 9.

Cut the cabbages into equal-size wedges, ensuring the core is kept intact. This will help keep the cabbage together as it braais. Drizzle the wedges with oil and season with salt and pepper.

Braai the wedges over high heat for 3 minutes per side on all three sides. Move the wedges to a cooler part of the grill and continue cooking for another 5 minutes, flipping the wedges occasionally to char evenly. Cook until they're tender but still have some crunch. Brush with Miso Butter on the last three turns before removing from the heat.

Arrange the wedges on a serving platter, drizzle with Miso Butter and sprinkle with dukkah. Serve with lemon wedges and devour.

WEST COAST BACON MUSSEL POT

Mussels are probably the most underrated seafood,
and they're one of our all-time favourites.

Feeds: 4 • Prep: 30 minutes • Cook: 20 minutes

---

200 g streaky bacon
A glug of oil for frying
1 large onion, peeled and chopped
2 cloves garlic, chopped
340 ml Darling Brew Bone Crusher
1 kg bag of sustainably farmed
  half-shell mussels
1 C fresh cream
A handful of fresh parsley, chopped
A handful of chopped fresh chives
A handful of chopped spring onions
Sea salt and freshly ground black pepper

Braai or fry the bacon slowly over medium heat. Flip the bacon occasionally so it cooks evenly and the fat renders out, leaving you with crispy bacon. Drain the bacon on kitchen towel, then roughly chop it.

Heat a big glug of oil in a number 3 potjie or a large flat-bottom pot over medium-heat coals. Add the onion and fry until it softens and browns. Add the garlic and fry for another minute until fragrant. Add the beer to the pot and bring it up to a boil. Toss in the mussels and steam with the lid on for 5 minutes.

Remove the pot from the heat and stir in the cream, parsley, chives and spring onions. Season to taste and serve with sprinkles of crispy bacon bits and plenty of bread to mop up the sauce.

Beer Pairing: Darling Brew Bone Crusher - beer in the pot and in the glass! With spicy, citrus flavours and hints of coriander and candied orange peel, witbiers are perfect with seafood. It's our favourite way to eat this tasty, sustainable seafood dish.

DB DARLING BREW

BLACKSMITH MUSHROOM BURGER

We first made these for our blacksmith mates
and they're just as good now as they were back then.

Feeds: 4 • Prep: 1 hour • Cook: 30 minutes

The Aubergines
2 large aubergines, sliced
Sea salt and freshly ground black pepper
A glug of oil for drizzling

The Pesto
Olive oil
100 g sundried tomato pesto

The Mushrooms
8 large, equal-size black mushrooms
1 large bag baby spinach
2 wheels camembert, sliced
Sea salt and freshly ground black pepper

Season the aubergines and drizzle with oil, then braai over medium-heat coals until cooked through.

Drizzle a little olive oil into the pesto to loosen it up, and season to taste.

To assemble your burgers, start with four big, flat mushrooms with the inside facing the sky. Next, lay down a bed of baby spinach, followed by two slices of aubergine. Top with three or four slices of the cheese, then add a large dollop of the pesto and spread it out. Season with salt and pepper, then top your masterpieces with a second mushroom, facing downwards. Secure the mushroom burgers with string like an old-school parcel.

Drizzle with oil and cook them slowly over medium-heat coals. When the mushrooms start to soften, they are close to done. Take them off and let them rest for 5 minutes if you can wait. Eating these monsters is a messy affair, so just do what the blacksmiths did and smash 'em in your face.

DARK CHOCOLATE AND BANANA BRAAIBROODJIES
WITH MAPLE SYRUP WHIPPED CREAM

These braaibroodjies have been known to convert non-banana-eating folk
into banana-devouring savages.

Feeds: 4-6 • Prep: 20 minutes • Cook: 15 minutes

The Broodjies
10 slices oat and honey bread
1 C melted butter
4-6 bananas (depending on size), sliced into rounds
1 slab Lindt 70% dark chocolate, grated
1 slab Lindt 70% dark chocolate, chopped

The Maple Syrup Whipped Cream
1 C whipping cream, cold
½ tsp vanilla essence
1 tsp ground cinnamon
¼ C maple syrup

To make the broodjies, spread out the bread slices, making sure each one has a partner, and brush with melted butter. Add the banana rounds in a layer and evenly sprinkle over the grated chocolate, followed by the chopped chocolate. Pop the tops on the sarmies, then brush both sides with butter and wrap them individually in foil.

To make the cream, whip the cream in a large bowl until peaks begin to form. Fold in the vanilla, cinnamon and maple syrup and whisk until stiff peaks form.

Put the foil-wrapped broodjies on the grid over medium-heat coals for about 5 minutes a side. This will melt all the goodness together inside the broodjies. Then take the broodjies out of the foil, arrange them in a flip grid and braai until golden brown. Serve with whipped cream and try not to eat them all before you share them with your mates.

STAGE 4: PLAN AHEAD

CHORIZO BBQ SLOPPY JOE BRAAIBROODJIES

This campfire classic gets a chorizo-infused braaibroodjie upgrade.

Makes: 8 broodjies • Prep: 20 minutes • Cook: 1 hour

The Mince

Olive oil
200 g chorizo, diced
1 large onion, peeled and chopped
1 small red pepper, deseeded and chopped
1 small yellow pepper, deseeded and chopped
1 small green pepper, deseeded and chopped
4 cloves garlic, chopped
1-2 red chillies, chopped
500 g beef mince
1 C Darling Brew Slow Beer
½ C tomato sauce

½ C Beer Country's Quarter Cup Braai Marinade
  (see p. 7) or your favourite BBQ sauce
¼ C Worcestershire sauce
Zest and juice of 1 small lemon
1 Tbsp sugar
Sea salt and freshly ground black pepper

The Broodjies

16 slices of white farm bread, buttered
  on both sides
250 g mozzarella, grated
250 g cheddar, grated

Preheat a large flat pot over medium-high-heat coals. Heat a splash of oil and add the chorizo. Stir-fry until the chorizo releases its oil, then add the onion and peppers. Fry for a few minutes until the veg begin to soften, then add the garlic and chilli and fry for another minute until fragrant. Toss in the mince and stir-fry until it has released all its moisture and starts to fry. Brown the mince off for a few minutes, then stir in the beer, tomato sauce, braai marinade or BBQ sauce and Worcestershire sauce. Bring to a boil and simmer, uncovered, for 20 minutes to reduce and thicken. If the mince is soupy, you'll end up with soggy broodjies. Add the lemon zest and juice, sugar, salt and pepper. Let the mince cool a bit before making the broodjies.

To make the broodjies, lay out half the bread slices on a work surface. Top each with mozzarella and a good amount of mince. Top with cheddar and a slice of bread. Braai the broodjies over medium-heat coals until golden brown and melty. Slice and serve them hot, then smash them!

Beer Pairing: Darling Brew Slow Beer - SA's original craft lager has a solid malt backbone to stand up to the meaty broodjies, and a bitter snap to cut through the cheesy richness. Its carbonation is light and easy, but strong enough to scrub the inside of your cheeks and get you ready for the next bite.

 DARLING BREW

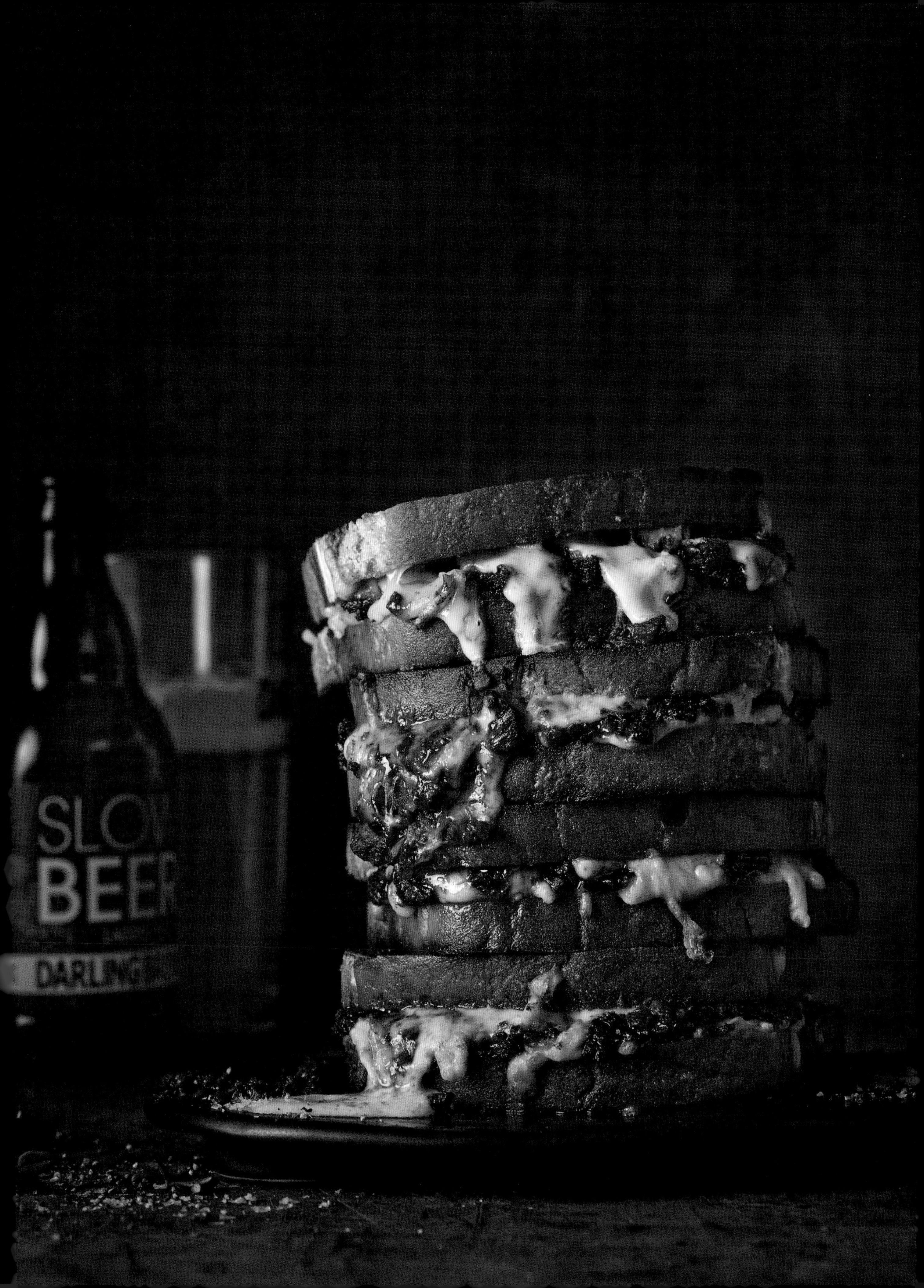
SLO
BEE
DARLING

MEGA STEAK ROLL
WITH FIERY GREEN PEPPERCORN SAUCE

The king of steak rolls has arrived, bend the knee!

Feeds: 4-6 • Prep: 20 minutes • Cook: 20 minutes

The Steak

700 g thick-cut rump steak
Olive oil
Sea salt, freshly ground black
  pepper or your favourite
  braai spice

The Fiery Green
Peppercorn Sauce

1 Tbsp olive oil
A knob of butter
1 small red onion, peeled and
  very finely chopped
3 cloves garlic, finely chopped

2 Tbsp green peppercorns
1 Tbsp crushed black
  peppercorns
¼ C brandy
1 C beef stock
1 C fresh cream
2 sprigs of fresh thyme,
  picked and chopped
Sea salt

The Mayo-Mustard

¼ C mayonnaise
¼ C Dijon mustard
Zest and juice of 1 small lemon

Sea salt and freshly ground
  black pepper

The Bread and Toppings

Butter
A large ciabatta, sliced
  horizontally
Wild rocket
Store-bought or homemade
  pickled onions (see p. 8)

Drizzle the steak with oil and season. Braai the steak over hot coals for 3-4 minutes per side or until the internal temperature hits 50 °C for medium-rare. Remove the steak from the heat and place it onto a plate to rest. Any resting juices will be added to the sauce later.

For the sauce, set a cast-iron pan over medium-heat coals. Heat the oil and butter and fry the onion until it softens and begins to brown. Add the garlic, green peppercorns and black peppercorns and fry for 2 minutes until fragrant. Pour in the brandy and use a lighter to ignite, but be careful. Let the brandy cook off, then pour in the beef stock, bring it to a boil and reduce it by half. Pour in the cream, thyme and any resting juices from the steak, then bring to a simmer. Cook until the sauce thickens enough to coat the back of a spoon. Move the pan to the side of the braai grid to keep warm.

Mix the ingredients for the mayo-mustard and season to taste.

Butter the ciabatta and braai until the buttered sides are golden all over. Set aside.

Slice the steak thinly and season with salt and pepper. To assemble, slather the mayo-mustard over the toasted sides of the bread, add a layer of wild rocket and pickled onions to the base. Top with slices of steak and spoon over the warm peppercorn sauce. Close up the loaf, slice it into four or six sarmies and serve with extra sauce on the side.

BLACK MUSHROOM AND BRIE BRAAIBROODJIES
WITH CHILLI CRISP

Get ready for an umami braaibroodjie bomb.

Makes: 5 braaibroodjies • Prep: 20 minutes • Cook: 25 minutes

---

The Mushrooms
Olive oil
A knob of butter
1 medium onion, peeled and chopped
500 g black mushrooms, sliced
3 cloves garlic, finely chopped
1 Tbsp chopped fresh thyme
¼ C soy sauce
Sea salt and freshly ground black pepper

The Broodjies
10 slices of white farm bread, buttered on both sides
250 g mozzarella, grated
250 g brie cheese, sliced
Chilli crisp
Sea salt and freshly ground black pepper

To make the mushrooms, set a cast-iron pan over medium-high heat. Heat a splash of olive oil and the butter, and fry the onion until it softens. Add the mushrooms and fry until they release their liquid and soften. Add the garlic and thyme and fry for another minute until fragrant. Pour in the soy sauce and fry until it has evaporated, then remove the pan from the heat. Season to taste and let the mixture cool.

To assemble, lay five slices of bread on your work surface and top with mozzarella. Add mushrooms to each slice, then the chilli crisp and finally the sliced brie. Season to taste. Top with a second slice of bread and transfer to a flip grid. Braai over medium-heat coals until golden and melty. Slice and serve with extra chilli crisp on the side.

COWBOY BUTTER STEAK
WITH ROOSTERKOEK

With a little forward thinking you'll enjoy the best steak roosterkoek of your life.

Feeds: 4-6 • Prep: Overnight + proofing time • Cook: 15 minutes

---

The Roosterkoek

500 g white bread wheat flour
350 g water
1 Tbsp olive oil
1 Tbsp sugar
10 g (1 packet) instant yeast
1 tsp salt

The Steak

Olive oil
800 g rump or sirloin
Sea salt and freshly ground black pepper
  and your favourite braai spice

The Cowboy Butter
(see p. 8)

If you followed the Make-ahead Dough recipe from the front of the book (see p. 8), take it out of the fridge at least 30 minutes before shaping. If you're starting from scratch, make sure you mix the dough for the roosterkoek at least 2 hours before you plan to braai.

If you're starting from scratch, mix all the ingredients for the dough in a large mixing bowl until no dry flour remains. Turn out the shaggy dough onto a work surface and knead for 8-10 minutes until the dough is soft and pliable. Place it back in the bowl and cover. Let it proof in a warm spot until it doubles in size.

Turn out the proofed dough onto a lightly floured work surface. Divide it into 10 pieces and shape into balls. Arrange the balls on a lightly floured tray and cover with a damp kitchen towel. Proof again for 30-40 minutes or until doubled in size.

Set up your fire with two coal zones, one hot and one medium. Oil the steak and season with salt and pepper or your favourite braai spice. Braai over hot coals for 4-5 minutes per side or until the internal temperature hits 50 °C for a medium-rare steak. Let the steak rest for 10 minutes before slicing. At the same time, braai the roosterkoek over medium-heat coals, turning frequently. When the roosterkoek sound hollow when tapped with a finger, they are done. Roosterkoek can take up to 20 minutes to bake, so plan accordingly.

To assemble, melt the Cowboy Butter slightly and slice the roosterkoek open. Top the roosterkoek with slices of steak, spoon over a generous amount of butter and ride off into a flavour sunset.

MONGOLIAN PORK NECK TACOS

Marinate these bad boys ahead of time and bask in the glory that is Mongolian pork tacos.

Feeds: 4-6 • Prep: Overnight • Cook: 15 minutes

The Marinade and Meat

Olive oil
4 cloves garlic, chopped
A knob of fresh ginger,
  peeled and chopped
2 red chillies, chopped
½ C soy sauce
¼ C rice vinegar
¼ C water
½ C brown sugar
¼ C gochujang paste
1 kg pork neck steaks

To Thicken the Sauce

1 tsp cornflour + 1 tsp water

To Serve

Flour tacos
Rainbow slaw mix
3 spring onions, sliced
2 Tbsp sesame seeds, toasted

Set a medium-size pot over medium-heat coals. Heat a glug of oil, add the garlic, ginger and chillies and stir-fry for 2 minutes until fragrant and starting to brown. Add the rest of the ingredients, except the pork, and stir well to combine and dissolve the sugar. Remove from the heat and let the mixture cool. Once cooled, pour it into a Ziploc bag and add the pork. Seal the bag, place it in a bowl and pop it in the fridge overnight.

The next day, remove the marinated meat from the fridge about an hour before you braai. Remove the pork from the marinade and pat it dry.

Pour the marinade into a large cast-iron pot, set it over medium heat and bring it to a boil. Simmer for 5 minutes. Mix the cornflour and water and stir it into the pot. Bring to a boil to thicken the marinade, then remove from the heat and set aside.

Braai the steaks over medium-hot coals for 3-4 minutes per side or until cooked to your liking. Let the steaks rest for at least 5 minutes before slicing and tossing in the sauce.

Warm the tacos on the grid and pop them into a pot with a lid to keep them warm.

To assemble, load up your flour tacos with sticky pork and top with rainbow slaw, spring onions and toasted sesame seeds.

SMOOR-SE-LEKKER ROOSTERKOEK BOERIES

There are boerie rolls and then there are these kickass *boeriekoek*.

Feeds: 4-6 • Prep: Overnight for dough + proofing time • Cook: 30 minutes

The Roosterkoek
(see p. 8 for Make-ahead Dough
  or see p. 53)

The Tomato Smoor
(see p. 6)

The Boeries
600 g thick wors

To Serve
Butter
Sea salt and freshly ground
  black pepper

If you followed the Make-ahead Dough recipe from the front of the book, take it out of the fridge at least 30 minutes before shaping. If you're starting from scratch, mix the roosterkoek dough at least 2 hours before you plan to braai.

If you're starting from scratch, follow the method on page 53.

While the roosterkoek are proofing, make the smoor (see method on page 6), then set aside.

Set up your fire in two zones: one medium-hot and one medium. Braai the wors over medium-hot coals until the exterior is caramelised and cooked to your liking. We like our wors a little pink in the middle. At the same time, braai the roosterkoek over medium-heat coals, turning frequently. When the roosterkoek sound hollow when tapped with a finger, they are done. Roosterkoek can take up to 20 minutes to bake, so plan accordingly.

To assemble, slice the roosterkoek open and butter generously. Top with wors and smoor, season to taste, and serve.

SEMI-DEBONED CHICKEN
WITH BASIL, CHIVES, LEMON AND GARLIC

Braaiing a whole chicken can take ages,
but this simple hack of removing the carcass is a game changer.

Feeds: 4-6 • Prep: 20 minutes • Cook: 30 minutes

The Marinade
A big handful of fresh basil, chopped
A handful of fresh chives, chopped
3 cloves garlic, chopped
¼ C olive oil
Zest and juice of 1 lemon
Sea salt and freshly ground black pepper

The Chicken
1.5 kg free-range chicken, room temperature
A sharp paring or boning knife
Sea salt and freshly ground black pepper

For the marinade, toss the basil, chives and garlic into a mortar and give it a bash with a pestle to combine. Add the olive oil, lemon zest and juice and season to taste. Give it a good mix and set it aside. If you don't have a pestle and mortar, just give it a chop and mix.

Deboning a chicken might seem tricky, but it just takes a little practice. We're only removing the carcass and the thigh bones, so think of it like taking a jacket off a hanger. Except the jacket is a chicken and the hanger is the carcass.

Start with the backbone facing up on your chopping board. Run a sharp knife along each side of the spine. Pick a side to start with, then run the tip of the knife in your initial cut and begin paring the meat off the carcass. Take your time with it, you'll get the feel for it. Slice through the thigh joint to release it from the carcass. You can snap the wing joints to make it easier to access the breast meat. Work the breast meat off the carcass until you've got the entire side off, then start on the other side. Once you've got both sides of the meat off the carcass, pull the carcass out and discard. Next, find the thigh bones and make a small cut on each side of the bones, then use your knife to work the bones free. Congratulations! You've just semi-deboned your first chicken.

Season the chicken on both sides with salt and pepper, then use three-quarters of the marinade and cover the chicken evenly. Place the bird skin-side down on a tray and fold it back into shape. This is how you're going to braai it. Transfer the chicken to a flip grid and braai over medium-hot coals for roughly 5 minutes per side for 20 minutes. At the 20-minute mark, brush the rest of the marinade on both sides of the chicken and braai for another 5 minutes per side. When the internal temperature hits 75 °C, it's done. Let the chicken rest for at least 10 minutes, then slice and serve.

DUKKAH-DUSTED
HARISSA WINGS

Two flavour heavyweights collide in these epic spicy wings.

Feeds: 4-6 • Prep: 20 minutes + overnight marinating (optional) • Cook: 30 minutes

---

The Wings

20 free-range chicken wings
A glug of oil for drizzling
Your favourite braai spice
Store-bought dukkah

The Harissa Marinade

3-5 tsp store-bought harissa paste
  (depending on how spicy you like it)
2 C double cream plain yoghurt
A squeeze of lime
Sea salt and freshly ground black pepper

Using a chef's knife or a pair of kitchen scissors, trim off the wing tip at the V of the joint of all the wings and discard.

Mix all the ingredients for the marinade and season to taste. Reserve half a cup of the marinade and coat the wings in the rest. Let the wings marinate overnight if you have time or for at least 1 hour.

If you marinated overnight, then pull the wings from the fridge at least 30 minutes before braaiing. Drizzle the wings with a little olive oil and season with your favourite braai spice.

Place the wings on a flip grid. Braai over medium-heat coals, flipping frequently for a total of 30 minutes. Baste with every turn to build up a tasty, caramelised crust. Pop the wings into your braaibak and toss them with the reserved marinade. Arrange the wings on a serving platter and top with a generous sprinkling of dukkah.

NACHO AVERAGE
TEX-MEX BURGERS

They're fresh, juicy, creamy and crunchy all in one bite. Yee-haw!

Feeds: 4 • Prep: 20 minutes • Cook: 15 minutes

The Pico De Gallo
300 g baby tomatoes, quartered
1 small red onion, peeled and chopped
1-2 pickled jalapeños, deseeded and chopped
Zest and juice of 1 lime
A handful of fresh coriander, chopped
Olive oil
Sea salt and freshly ground black pepper

The Avo
2 avocados
A squeeze of lime juice
Sea salt and freshly ground black pepper

The Patties and Toppings
4 good quality free-range
  beef burger patties
Olive oil
Your favourite braai spice
8 slices of mozzarella or cheddar
Butter
4 good quality burger rolls
1 large packet of BBQ Big Korn Bites

For the pico de gallo, add the tomatoes, onion, jalapeños, lime zest and juice and coriander to a bowl. Drizzle with olive oil to coat, then season to taste and mix well. Cover and pop it in the fridge until needed.

Peel and smash the avos in a small bowl, add the lime juice and season to taste. Cover and place in the fridge until needed.

Drizzle the patties with oil and season with your favourite braai spice. Braai the patties over hot coals for 2-3 minutes per side or until cooked to your liking. Just before you're going to remove the patties from the braai, place the mozzarella or cheddar on the patties and cover them with a braaibak. This will create steam to melt the cheese. Once the cheese is melted, remove the patties from the heat and set aside to rest while you butter and toast the buns.

To assemble, give each roll base a dollop of avo. Add the patties, top with pico de gallo, a handful of Big Korn Bites and the top half of the roll. Tuck in.

ROAST BEETROOT
WITH LEMON LABNEH AND PISTACHIOS

We've always loved roast beetroot and you'll love this earthy,
creamy and nutty flavour bomb.

Feeds: 4-6 • Prep: 10 minutes • Cook: 1 hour

The Labneh
(see p. 9)

The Beetroot
6 beetroots, washed
Olive oil
Sea salt and freshly ground black pepper

To Serve
Olive oil
Sea salt and freshly ground black pepper
100 g pistachios, chopped

Make the Labneh by following the instructions on page 9.

Drizzle the washed beetroots with olive oil and season with salt and pepper. Wrap each beetroot in foil and place them into the medium-heat coals. Cook for 45 minutes, then check to see if the beetroots are tender by sticking a fork into them. If it slides in easily to the centre, they are cooked. If not, give them another 10 minutes, then check again.

When the beets are cooked, remove them from the foil and let them cool until you can handle them. Slice the beets into quarters.

To assemble, spoon the Labneh onto a serving platter and swirl it around to create a base. Arrange the warm beets on top, drizzle with olive oil and season to taste. Top with pistachios and serve.

BRAAIED SWEET POTATO WEDGES
WITH GREEN HERB SAUCE AND PERI-PERI DIPPING LABNEH

These braaied sweet spuds are perfect on their own or as a great side to any main.

Feeds: 4-6 • Prep: 10 minutes • Cook: 45 minutes

The Peri-Peri Labneh
1 C Labneh (see p. 9)
¼ C store-bought peri-peri sauce
Sea salt and freshly ground black pepper

The Green Herb Sauce
(see p. 7)

The Wedges
6 large sweet potatoes
Olive oil
Your favourite braai spice

For the peri-peri labneh, follow the instructions on page 9 to make the Labneh. Stir in the peri-peri sauce and season to taste.

Make the Green Herb Sauce by following the instructions on page 7.

Slice the sweet potatoes into wedges but keep the sections together (you're going to put them back together before you wrap them in foil). Drizzle the wedges with oil and season with your favourite braai spice. Put the wedges back together to form each potato and wrap in foil. Place the wrapped potatoes onto the grid or into the coals and cook until tender but not falling apart.

Remove the potatoes from the grid and carefully unwrap them. Place the wedges into a flip grid and pop it back onto the fire. Brown the potatoes on both sides until caramelised and charry.

Arrange the wedges on a serving platter and drizzle with Green Herb Sauce.

Serve the wedges with the peri-peri labneh for dipping, and tuck in.

CHARRED GREENS
WITH LABNEH, SMOOR, DUKKAH AND PARMESAN

*Charred and crunchy with luscious labneh,
a sexy smoor and a sprinkling of the good stuff. Mama mia!*

Feeds: 4-6 • Prep: 10 minutes + 20 minutes for marinating • Cook: 45 minutes

---

The Marinade
2 Tbsp olive oil
2 Tbsp soy sauce
2 cloves garlic, finely chopped
1 tsp chilli flakes

The Greens
10 pieces of tenderstem broccoli
8 baby marrows, halved lengthways
6 spring onions

To Serve
Labneh (see p. 9)
Tomato Smoor (see p. 6)
¼ C grated parmesan
Zest of 1 lemon
Store-bought dukkah
Sea salt and freshly ground black pepper

Mix all the ingredients for the marinade in a large bowl, then add the greens and toss. Let the greens marinate for 20 minutes.

Arrange the greens in a flip grid and braai over medium-hot coals for 2-3 minutes per side. You want the greens to be charry and tender while still retaining some bite.

To assemble, arrange the greens on a serving platter and add dollops of labneh and smoor. Top with grated parmesan, lemon zest and dukkah, then season to taste and serve.

COCONUT PANNA COTTA
WITH GRILLED PINEAPPLE AND TOASTED COCONUT

The perfect get-ahead load-shedding dessert.

Makes: 6-8 • Prep: 20 minutes • Cook: 15 minutes

The Panna Cotta
3 Tbsp cold water
1 packet (10 g) gelatine
2 C double cream yoghurt
1 tin (400 ml) coconut milk
  + 100 ml milk
2 tsp vanilla essence
½ C white sugar

The Pineapple
Olive oil
1 small pineapple, peeled and
  sliced into rounds

The Toppings
Coconut flakes, toasted
Honey

Place 6-8 tumbler glasses or small bowls onto a baking tray that fits into your fridge.

For the panna cotta, mix the water and gelatine together in a small bowl and set aside to bloom. Add the yoghurt to a large jug or bowl and set aside. Pour the coconut milk, milk, vanilla essence and sugar into a medium-size pot. Set over medium heat and warm to melt the sugar. Remove from the heat when the sugar is dissolved, add the bloomed gelatine and whisk to combine.

Pour the warm mixture into the yoghurt, while whisking, until completely combined. Pour the mixture evenly into the glasses, then place in the fridge for at least 4 hours or overnight to set.

Remove the panna cottas from the fridge before you braai the pineapples just to take off the chill. Brush the pineapple with olive oil and grill, on both sides for 4-5 minutes until charry and semi-soft. Remove from the heat and slice into smaller pieces.

To assemble, top each panna cotta with grilled pineapple, toasted coconut and a drizzle of honey. Serve and smash them!

STAGE 6: WEEKEND WINNERS

FALL-OFF-THE-BONE MONKEY GLAND POTJIE RIBS

We ain't monkeying around with these ribs.

Feeds: 4-6 • Prep: 20 minutes • Cook: up to 2½ hours

The Monkey Gland
Oil for frying
1 large onion, peeled and
  sliced vertically
50 g butter
4 cloves garlic, chopped
A knob of ginger, chopped
1 C tomato sauce
1 C chutney
1 C stout
¼ C Worcestershire sauce
2 Tbsp honey
2 Tbsp brown vinegar
1 Tbsp soy sauce
1 Tbsp Tabasco sauce

The Ribs
2 racks of pork spare or loin ribs
Olive oil
Your favourite braai spice

To Serve
2 spring onions, thinly sliced
Lime wedges or slices

For the monkey gland sauce, preheat a medium-size flat pot or a number 3 potjie over medium-heat coals. Add a splash of oil and fry the onion until it is soft and starting to brown. Add the butter, garlic and ginger and fry for a minute until fragrant. Add the remaining sauce ingredients and stir to combine. Simmer the sauce with the lid off until reduced by a third - about 10 minutes.

Drizzle the ribs with oil and season with braai spice. Braai the ribs over medium-hot coals for a few minutes on both sides. The idea is not to cook the ribs through, but rather to caramelise the exterior so that they're nice and charry. Remove the ribs from the braai and slice them into two rib pieces.

Toss the ribs in the sauce, then stand them on their sides and arrange them in the pot. Place the lid on and bring to a simmer. Braise the ribs slowly over medium-low coals for 1 hour. At the 1-hour mark, check the ribs for tenderness. If they need more time, give them another 30-60 minutes, then check again. The meat should be almost falling off the bone. Give the ribs a final basting of sauce and season to taste. Serve them straight out of the pot with lime wedges or slices for squeezing.

BRAAIED BUTTER CHICKEN CURRY

Butter chicken seems to be the universal curry that everyone loves, and for good reason. It's so damn tasty, and this version takes things to a whole new braai level.

Feeds: 6-8 • Prep: Overnight + 30 minutes • Cook: 1 hour + resting time

The Chicken
1½ C double cream yoghurt
3 cloves garlic, finely chopped
A big knob of fresh ginger, finely chopped
2 Tbsp garam masala
2 Tbsp Kashmiri chilli powder
1 Tbsp ground cumin
2 tsp ground turmeric
A squeeze of lemon juice
Sea salt and freshly ground black pepper
2 kg deboned and skinned chicken thighs
6 kebab sticks

The Potjie
Oil for frying
A big knob of butter
2 large onions, peeled and chopped
3 cloves garlic, finely chopped
A knob of fresh ginger, finely chopped
1 Tbsp Kashmiri chilli powder
1 Tbsp garam masala
1 Tbsp ground cumin
½ Tbsp ground coriander
2 C tomato purée
2 Tbsp fish sauce
1 Tbsp brown sugar
100 g crème fraîche
1 tsp crushed dried fenugreek leaves (you'll have to visit a spice shop for these)
Sea salt and freshly ground black pepper

To Serve
Naan bread or basmati rice
¼ C almond flakes, toasted
Fresh coriander

To make the chicken, mix all the ingredients, except the chicken and kebab sticks, in a container with a lid. Add the chicken and give it a good massage, then refrigerate to marinate overnight. The next day, remove the container from the fridge and allow it to come to room temperature.

Thread the chicken onto the kebab sticks and braai over very hot coals. You are not trying to cook the chicken through, you just need to char and caramelise it. Brush each kebab with extra marinade at each turn, then set aside when you are happy with them. Allow to cool before removing the chicken from the kebab sticks. At this point you can cut the chicken pieces into small pieces or leave as they are.

To make the potjie, preheat a number 3 potjie over medium-high-heat coals. Add a splash of oil and the knob of butter and fry the onions until they soften and start to brown. Add the garlic and ginger and fry for a minute until fragrant. Toss in all the spices and fry for another minute. Stir in the tomato purée, fish sauce and sugar. Bring to a simmer over low-heat coals for 20 minutes to let the flavours make friends.

This step is optional, but it does give you that awesome curry house gravy result. After 20 minutes, remove the pot from the heat and use a hand blender to blitz the curry sauce until smooth. Return the pot to the heat and add the chicken. Stir in the crème fraîche and fenugreek leaves and simmer for another 15 minutes to cook the chicken. Season to taste, then remove the pot from the heat, cover and let it rest for 10 minutes before serving. Serve it with naan bread or basmati rice with a sprinkle of toasted almonds and fresh coriander.

SMOKY BEER CHILLI
WITH CORIANDER LIME SOUR CREAM

Chilli is good for breakfast, lunch or dinner and this version will change your life.

Feeds: 6-8 • Prep: 1 hour • Cook: 2 hours

The Coriander Lime Sour Cream
1 C sour cream
1 large ripe avocado, peeled and mashed
A small handful of fresh coriander, chopped
A small handful of chopped spring onion
A squeeze of lime juice
A pinch of lime zest
Sea salt and freshly ground black pepper

The Chilli
2 kg chuck steak
Sea salt and freshly ground black pepper

A glug of oil for drizzling
2 large onions, peeled and finely chopped
2 red peppers, finely chopped
5 cloves garlic, finely chopped
5 anchovy fillets, chopped
2-3 Tbsp chilli powder (adjust to taste)
2 Tbsp ground cumin
2 Tbsp ground coriander
2 Tbsp paprika
2 Tbsp smoked paprika
2 tsp garlic powder
½ C gherkin brine (the juice in the gherkin bottle)
2-3 smoked chipotles or fresh chillies, chopped (adjust to taste)

2 tins (400 g each) chopped tomatoes
1 C tomato sauce
1 pot or sachet of beef stock concentrate
2 C coffee stout
1 tin (400 g) red kidney beans, rinsed and drained
1 punnet baby tomatoes, left whole

To Serve
Grated mature cheddar
Santa Anna's corn chips

To make the sour cream, mix all the ingredients together and blitz with a hand blender. Keep it in the fridge until you are ready to serve.

To make the chilli, season the chuck with salt and pepper and drizzle with oil. Sear over very hot coals for 1-2 minutes per side. Allow the meat to rest for 5 minutes before removing it from the bone. Cube the meat and keep the bones for the pot for extra flavour.

In a number 3 potjie, use a good splash of oil and fry the onions until they soften and brown. Add the red peppers, garlic and anchovies and fry for a minute until fragrant. Add the chilli powder, cumin, coriander, paprika, smoked paprika and garlic powder and fry for another 2 minutes to cook out the spices. Deglaze the pan with gherkin brine. Add the cubed meat and don't forget the bones. Add the chillies, tomatoes, tomato sauce, stock and beer.

Simmer with the lid off over medium-low heat for 1½ hours. Add the kidney beans and baby tomatoes and simmer for another 30 minutes. Remove the bones. Top with grated cheddar and serve hot with plenty of corn chips for scooping and sour cream to chill the burn.

BEEF AND PUMPKIN POT
WITH FETA HERB DUMPLINGS

The potjie is delicious, meaty and earthy, but the dumplings are the real kicker.

Feeds: 6-8 • Prep: 45 minutes • Cook: 2½ hours

The Potjie
2 kg beef shin (bone-in)
A glug of oil for frying
Sea salt and freshly ground black pepper
1 large onion, peeled and chopped
2 cloves garlic, chopped
2 tsp ground cumin
1 tsp ground cinnamon
5 anchovies, finely chopped
A handful of fresh thyme, picked and chopped
A handful of fresh sage, chopped
2 C pumpkin ale or amber ale
1 C good-quality beef stock

1 Tbsp cornflour, dissolved in 1 Tbsp water
1 kg diced pumpkin
12 baby onions, peeled

The Feta Herb Dumplings
500 g cake wheat flour
2 tsp baking powder
1½ tsp salt
100 g butter
100 g feta, crumbled
1 Tbsp chopped fresh thyme
1 Tbsp chopped fresh sage
1¼ C cold water

Drizzle the meat with oil and season with salt and pepper. Braai over a hot fire for a couple of minutes a side to brown it. Once the meat has cooled enough to work with, cut it into bite-size chunks. Keep the bones with the marrow for extra flavour.

Heat a glug of oil in a flat-bottom potjie and fry the chopped onion until soft and brown. Add the garlic, cumin, cinnamon and anchovies and fry for another minute. Add the meat, bones, thyme and sage to the pot, then pour in the pumpkin or amber ale and stock. Simmer with the lid on for 1 hour.

Stir in the cornflour and water. Add the pumpkin and baby onions and stir to combine. This is the last time you are going to stir the pot. Pop on the lid and cook for another 45 minutes. In the meantime, make the dumpling dough.

For the dumplings, mix the flour, baking powder and salt. Rub in the butter with your fingertips, then add the feta and herbs. Add the cold water and mix until the dough comes together. Turn the dough out onto a lightly floured surface. Divide the dough into golf ball-size pieces and lightly roll them into balls.

At the 45-minute mark, open the lid of the pot and place the dough balls on top of the liquid. Cover, spread some coals on the top of the lid and cook for 30 minutes. Check the dumplings after 30 minutes and if they need more colour, then add more coals to the lid and cook for another 5-10 minutes. Remove the pot from the heat and let it rest uncovered for at least 10 minutes before serving.

IRISH-ISH OXTAIL STOUT POTJIE

Inspired by the dark, rich soil and rolling green hills of the Emerald Isle, here's our potjie take on an Irish classic.

Feeds: 8 • Prep: 30 minutes • Cook: 4½ hours + standing time

The Braai

2 kg oxtail
300 g Brussels sprouts, halved
4 leeks, washed
Oil for drizzling
Sea salt and freshly ground black pepper

The Potjie

Oil for frying
1 large onion, peeled and finely chopped
1 stalk celery, finely chopped
1 large carrot, grated
50 g butter
3 cloves garlic, finely chopped
A handful of fresh thyme, picked
   and finely chopped

A handful of fresh sage, finely chopped
2 sprigs of fresh rosemary, picked
   and finely chopped
50 g tomato paste
2 C stout
2 C good-quality beef stock
2 Tbsp chutney
1 Tbsp balsamic vinegar
1 Tbsp fish sauce
1 Tbsp cornflour, dissolved in 1 Tbsp water

To Serve

Finely sliced leeks (optional)
Colcannon or crusty bread

Drizzle the oxtail, Brussels sprouts and leeks with oil and season with salt and pepper. Braai the oxtail over hot coals until the exterior is well caramelised. Set aside. Braai the Brussels sprouts and leeks in a flip grid until charred. Once cooled, slice the leeks into rounds.

To make the potjie, preheat a number 3 potjie over medium-high-heat coals. Add a splash of oil and fry the onion, celery and carrot until softened and browned. Add the butter, garlic and herbs and fry for a minute until fragrant. Next, add the tomato paste and fry for a few minutes to caramelise. Add the oxtail and give the pot a good stir. Pour in the stout to deglaze the pot, then stir in the stock, chutney, balsamic vinegar and fish sauce. Put on the lid and simmer for 3½ hours.

At the 3½-hour mark, check the oxtail for tenderness. If it is still a little tough, give it another 30 minutes, then check again. When the meat is tender, but not falling off the bone, gently stir in the cornflour and water and add the charred leeks and the Brussels sprouts. Simmer uncovered for 30 minutes. Remove the pot from the heat and allow to stand for 15 minutes with the lid on.

Garnish with finely sliced leeks, if you like. Serve with traditional colcannon or crusty bread on the side and down it with a pint of the black stuff.

MOJO POTJIE PULLED PORK
WITH YOGHURT FLATBREADS

Inspired by the movie *Chef*, this porky crowd-pleaser is the perfect weekend project.

Feeds: 6-8 • Prep: Overnight • Cook: 3 hours

The Marinade and Pork
½ C olive oil
1 C orange juice
Zest of 1 orange
Zest and juice of 3 limes
1 handful each of fresh
    coriander and mint, chopped
1 head of garlic, chopped
2 Tbsp fish sauce
1 Tbsp dried oregano
1 Tbsp ground cumin
2 tsp chilli flakes
½ tsp sea salt
1 tsp freshly ground
    black pepper

2.5 kg boneless pork shoulder,
    butterflied

The Potjie
½ C Gypsy Mask Native Ale
½ C Beer Country's Quarter Cup
    Braai Marinade (see p. 7)
1 handful each of fresh
    coriander and mint, chopped
    (to add once the meat has
    been shredded)

The Flatbreads
300 g cake wheat flour
250 g double cream yoghurt

1 Tbsp baking powder
1 clove garlic, finely chopped
1 tsp salt
Zest of 1 lime
Flour for dusting
Melted butter for brushing

To Serve
1 small red cabbage, shredded
3 spring onions, sliced
Yoghurt Pesto (see p. 7)
Chilli crisp

Combine the olive oil, orange juice and zest, lime juice and zest, the chopped coriander and mint, garlic, fish sauce, dried oregano, ground cumin, chilli flakes, sea salt and black pepper, and pour into a large Ziploc bag. Pop the pork into the bag, seal and give it a good shake, then place it into a bowl and put it in the fridge. After 12-24 hours remove the pork from the marinade and pour the marinade, ale and Beer Country's Quarter Cup Braai Marinade into a number 3 potjie.

Brown the pork over medium-hot coals until the exterior is caramelised. Pop the pork into the potjie and baste it with the sauce. Bring the potjie to a simmer, then cook slowly over medium-low coals for around 3 hours. When the pork hits an internal temperature of 95 ºC, it's done. Remove the potjie from the heat and let the pork rest in the sauce while you prepare the flatbreads.

Mix all the flatbread ingredients (except the flour for dusting and the melted butter) in a large mixing bowl until the dough comes together. Don't knead it to death; just work it until it forms a ball and is not too sticky. Turn out the dough onto a floured surface, dust with a little flour and divide the dough into 10 balls. Flour the balls and roll out into circles, just smaller than a dinner plate. Braai or fry them in a dry pan for roughly 2 minutes per side, brushing with the melted butter when you flip them. Pop the cooked flatbreads into a pot with a lid to keep them warm as you go.

Using forks, shred the pork into the sauce, season to taste then sprinkle in the chopped coriander and mint. Serve on flatbreads with red cabbage, spring onions, Yoghurt Pesto and chilli crisp.

Beer Pairing: Darling Brew Gypsy Mask - the rich sweetness from the amber malts and subtle hop spice is the perfect contrast to this umami bomb of meat, spice and herbs. It finishes on a moderately bitter note that leaves you wanting more.

SEASIDE BUNNY CHOWS

Born out of necessity, Durban's most famous food export is up there with the finest meals you'll ever eat. Take a bow, Mr Bunny Chow; you're a true local food champion.

Feeds: 6-8 • Prep: 30 minutes • Cook: 3 hours

The Braai
2 kg lamb shoulder, deboned and butterflied
Oil for drizzling
Sea salt and freshly ground black pepper

The Potjie
¼ C oil
2 large onions, peeled and chopped
4 whole cloves
1 large stick cinnamon
2 star anise
2 cardamom pods, bruised
3 bay leaves
2 Tbsp tomato paste
4 cloves garlic, finely chopped
1 large knob of ginger, finely chopped
1 Tbsp ground cumin
1 Tbsp ground coriander

2 tsp ground turmeric
2-3 Tbsp Durban masala
2 Tbsp Kashmiri chilli powder
15 curry leaves
3 whole green chillies, tops cut off
2 C tomato purée
1 Tbsp brown sugar
2 C hot water
Sea salt and freshly ground black pepper
2 Tbsp garam masala
4 large potatoes, peeled and halved
2 Tbsp crème fraîche

To Serve
2 loaves of white farm bread,
   cut into quarters and hollowed out
Fresh coriander, chopped
Grated carrot, tossed in lemon juice

Slice the lamb shoulder into chunks that are big enough not to fall through a flip grid. Give the lamb a good drizzle of oil and season with salt and pepper. Place the lamb into the flip grid and braai it over hot coals for a couple of minutes to caramelise the exterior, then set aside. If you want to cut the lamb into bite-size chunks, now is a good time to do it.

To make the potjie, preheat a number 3 potjie over medium-high-heat coals. Add the oil, then the onions, cloves, cinnamon, star anise, cardamom and bay leaves. Fry for 6-8 minutes, while stirring, until the onions are soft and beginning to brown. Add the tomato paste, garlic, ginger, cumin, coriander, turmeric, masala, chilli powder, curry leaves and chillies and stir-fry for 2 minutes until fragrant. Stir in the tomato purée, sugar, water, salt and pepper. Add the lamb to the pot and give it a good stir. Pop on the lid and simmer for 1½ hours.

At the 1½-hour mark, taste the curry for seasoning. Next, sprinkle the garam masala over the top, add the potatoes and continue cooking with the lid open a crack for another 30 minutes. After 30 minutes, gently stir the crème fraîche into the curry.

Now build your bunnies, and always remember, never skimp on the gravy! Top each with fresh coriander and grated carrot.

AUBERGINE PARMIGIANA

Charred aubergine, rich tomato basil sauce and melty cheese: what's not to love?

Feeds: 4-6 • Prep: 20 minutes • Cook: 1 hour

The Aubergine
8 medium-size aubergines, sliced
  lengthways into 1 cm-thick pieces
Olive oil
Sea salt and freshly ground black pepper

The Tomato Sauce
Olive oil
A knob of butter
1 large onion, peeled and chopped
4 cloves garlic, chopped
4 anchovies, chopped
1 Tbsp dried oregano
2 sprigs of fresh rosemary, picked and chopped
¼ C baby capers, roughly chopped
¼ C red wine vinegar

2 tins (400 g each) good quality whole
  peeled tomatoes, crushed by hand
1 C water
A big knob of butter
A small handful of fresh basil,
  roughly chopped
Sea salt and freshly ground black pepper

The Cheese and Basil
300 g grated mozzarella
200 g grated parmesan
A small handful of fresh basil, roughly chopped

To Serve
Green Herb Sauce (see p. 7)

Drizzle the aubergines with olive oil and season with salt and pepper. Braai the aubergines over hot coals until they soften and start to char. Remove from the heat and set aside.

For the sauce, preheat a large flat pot over medium-high-heat coals. Add a splash of olive oil, then toss in the butter and onion. Fry until the onion softens and browns, then add the garlic, anchovies, oregano, rosemary and capers and stir-fry for 2 minutes until fragrant. Deglaze with the red wine vinegar and add the tomatoes and water. Bring to a simmer and cook, uncovered, for around 20 minutes or until the liquid has reduced by about half. Remove the pot from the heat and add the butter and fresh basil, stirring to combine. Transfer the sauce to another bowl so that you can build the aubergine parmigiana in the pot and not have to worry about cleaning it.

To assemble, add a thin layer of sauce to the pot and spread it evenly. Add a layer of aubergine, then top with sauce and a little mozzarella and grated parmesan. Repeat this process, adding the second handful of chopped basil to one of the middle layers for a herbaceous kick, until you've used all the ingredients. Season the middle layer with salt and pepper. Give the top a liberal sprinkling of cheese, then pop on the lid.

Use a spade to create a circular space in the coals for the pot. Place the pot into the space, then surround it with medium-low-heat coals. Spread some coals on the lid and bake for 30-40 minutes or until bubbly and browned. Alternatively, if the power comes back on, bake in the oven, uncovered, at 200 °C for 30-35 minutes until golden. Let it rest for 10 minutes before slicing and serving with Green Herb Sauce.

POTJIE BBQ LAMB RIBBETJIES
WITH MINT LABNEH

Sweet and sticky ribbetjies on a punchy mint labneh base.

Feeds: 4-6 • Prep: 20 minutes • Cook: 1 hour

The Mint Labneh
2 C Labneh (see p. 9)
A big handful of fresh mint, chopped
2 cloves garlic, chopped
1 red chilli, chopped
1 tsp ground cumin
Zest and juice of 1 lemon
Sea salt and freshly ground black pepper

The Pot
1 C Beer Country's Quarter Cup
  Braai Marinade (see p. 7)
1 C lager

The Ribbetjies
1 kg lamb ribbetjies
Olive oil
Your favourite braai spice

To Serve
Chilli crisp

For the mint labneh, mix all the ingredients in a bowl. Season to taste, cover and place it in the fridge until needed.

For the pot, pour the marinade and beer into a large flat pot or number 3 potjie. Pop it on the fire and bring it to a simmer, then remove it from the heat.

Drizzle the ribbetjies with oil and season with your favourite braai spice. Braai the ribbetjies over medium-hot coals to caramelise and char on all sides. You are not cooking them through, you're just browning the exterior. Remove the ribbetjies from the heat and place them into the pot with the marinade and lager. Mix well to coat them in the marinade, then place the pot back over medium-low coals. Cover and simmer for 45 minutes. After 45 minutes, remove the lid and continue simmering to reduce the sauce. When the lamb is tender, remove the pot from the fire and let the meat rest for 10 minutes.

To assemble, scoop the labneh onto a large serving platter and use the back of a spoon to spread it out. Arrange the warm ribbetjies on the labneh, then drizzle with marinade and garnish as desired. Season to taste and serve it up with chilli crisp!

LAMB BOBOTIE
WITH COCONUT PANGRATTATO

A nostalgic flavour bomb with aromatic spices from our mates at Cape Herb & Spice, and a crunchy coconut twist.

Feeds: 6 • Prep: 20 minutes • Cook: 1 hour

The Bobotie

2 slices of white bread, crusts removed
½ C milk
Oil for frying
2 medium onions, peeled and chopped
1 stick cinnamon
2 whole cloves
2 bay leaves
1 kg lamb mince
4 Tbsp Cape Herb & Spice Cape Malay Curry Spice
1 Tbsp ground cumin
1 Tbsp ground coriander
2 tsp ground turmeric
1 tsp chilli flakes
4 cloves garlic, finely chopped
1 large knob of fresh ginger, finely chopped
¼ C malt vinegar
¼ C chutney
2 green apples, grated
½ C sultanas or raisins or a mix
A small handful of fresh flat-leaf parsley, chopped
A squeeze of lemon juice
3 eggs
1 C fresh cream
Extra bay leaves for decoration

The Coconut Pangrattato

2 Tbsp olive oil
½ C panko breadcrumbs
¼ C desiccated coconut
½ tsp garlic powder
Zest of 1 lemon
Sea salt and freshly ground black pepper

To make the bobotie, tear the bread into pieces and soak it in the milk. Heat a large flat pot over medium-high-heat coals and add a glug of oil. Add the onions, cinnamon stick, whole cloves and bay leaves and fry for 5 minutes until the onions soften and brown. Add the mince and fry until any liquid has cooked out and you hear it start to sizzle and brown. Once browned, add the spices and fry for a couple of minutes until fragrant. Add the garlic and ginger and stir-fry for a minute until fragrant. Add the malt vinegar to deglaze the pot and fry for another minute.

Remove the pot from the heat and stir in the chutney, apples, raisins, parsley and lemon juice. Squeeze the milk from the bread and add the bread to the pot, mixing well to combine.

Flatten the mixture evenly in the pot and allow to cool slightly. Whisk the eggs and cream together, then pour it over the mince. Top with a few bay leaves, then cover. Use a spade to create a clear circular space in the coals for the pot. Place the pot into the space, then surround it with medium-low-heat coals, ensuring that no coals touch the pot. Spread a few coals on the lid and bake for 30-40 minutes. Alternatively, if the power comes back on, bake in the oven, uncovered, at 180 °C for 30-35 minutes until golden.

While the bobotie bakes, mix the pangrattato ingredients and tip them into a dry non-stick frying pan. Stir-fry over medium heat until golden. Serve the bobotie with sprinkles of pangrattato.

BLACK MIST STICKY TOFFEE PUDDING

The British classic gets a Darling Brew upgrade.

Feeds: 6 • Prep: 20 minutes • Cook: 30 minutes

The Dates

250 ml Darling Brew Black Mist
200 g dates, pitted and chopped
1 tsp bicarbonate of soda

The Wet

200 g butter, softened
200 g treacle sugar
2 Tbsp golden syrup
1 Tbsp vanilla essence
4 large eggs

The Dry

300 g cake wheat flour
1 Tbsp baking powder
2 tsp ground ginger
1 tsp salt

The Toffee Sauce

100 g butter
80 g treacle sugar
¼ C golden syrup

1 C fresh cream, room
  temperature
A big pinch of sea salt to
  taste

To Serve

250 ml Woolworths Ayrshire
  double thick cream
  or mascarpone
Chopped walnuts, toasted

Pop the stout and dates into a small pot and bring to a boil. Add the bicarb and let it foam up, then cook for a minute or so until it stops foaming. Remove from the heat. Roughly mash with a fork, then set aside to cool.

For the wet, add the butter and sugar to a mixing bowl and mix well with a spatula to combine. Mix in the syrup, vanilla and eggs, then set aside.

Grease a medium-size flat-bottom pot with butter. Prepare medium-heat coals, then create a circular space in the coals for the pot. Preheat the pot for 10 minutes while you mix the dry ingredients.

For the dry, add the flour, baking powder, ground ginger and salt to a mixing bowl and whisk to combine, then tip into the wet. Add the dates and fold with a spatula until well combined with no dry flour. Pour the batter into the preheated flat pot and put on the lid. Place the pot into the prepared space and surround it with medium-heat coals. Bake for 20 minutes, then place some coals on the lid and continue baking for another 10-15 minutes. Alternatively, if the power comes back on, pop it into the oven at 180 °C for 30 minutes. Stick a toothpick into the centre - if it comes out clean it's cooked.

Meanwhile, make the sauce. Melt the butter, sugar and syrup in a small pot. Whisk in the cream and bring to a boil. Simmer for 6-8 minutes or until the sauce turns a caramel colour. Season with salt, remove from the heat. Prick the baked pudding all over with a toothpick and pour over half the caramel sauce. Let it sit for a few minutes to absorb the sauce, then add the rest. Serve up the pudding with double thick cream or mascarpone and toasted walnuts.

Beer Pairing: Darling Brew Black Mist - packed with the chocolate and coffee flavours of dark malt, this brew is not only in the pudding, but it also pairs brilliantly with it. It cuts through the hefty date-soaked toffee pudding with ease and adds extra layers of roasted flavour along the way.

CHOCOLATE AND HAZELNUT BROWNIE BREAD
WITH BERRIES AND ICE CREAM

Slice it thick and pile it high with toppings for the best results.

Feeds: 6-8 • Prep: 20 minutes • Cook: 55 minutes

The Brownie

150 g cake wheat flour
100 g hazelnuts, toasted, cooled and chopped
1 tsp baking powder
1 tsp salt
150 g 70% dark chocolate,
  chopped into bite-size pieces
4 large eggs
100 g cocoa powder

1 Tbsp vanilla essence
2 tsp instant coffee granules
200 g butter
400 g brown sugar

To Serve

Vanilla ice cream
Fresh berries
Cocoa powder, for dusting

Use a spade to create a clear circular space in the coals for the pot. Place a flat pot into the space and surround it with medium-low-heat coals, ensuring that no coals touch the pot. Let the pot preheat while you mix the batter.

Line a loaf tin with baking paper and set aside.

Add the flour, hazelnuts, baking powder, salt and chocolate to a mixing bowl and mix to combine. To another mixing bowl, add the eggs, cocoa powder, vanilla and coffee and whisk to combine.

Set a pot over medium-heat coals. Add the butter and allow it to melt, then add the sugar. Stir and cook until bubbles start to form around the edges. Remove from the heat and pour it into the egg mixture, whisking until it's smooth and glossy.

Pour the dry ingredients into the chocolate mixture and, using a spatula, fold to combine until there is no dry flour.

Pour the batter into the loaf tin and carefully place it into the preheated flat pot. Put on the lid and place a few coals on the lid. Bake for 50-55 minutes. To check if it is done, stick a toothpick into the centre and if it comes out mostly clean it's cooked. Alternatively, if the power comes back on, pop it into the oven at 180 °C for 50-55 minutes.

Remove the tin from the pot and let it cool for at least 20 minutes before using the baking paper to lift it out. Slice and serve with scoops of ice cream, fresh berries and a dusting of cocoa powder.

RECIPE INDEX